This journal belongs to

_____

Date

_____

To Bach there was no difference between sacred and secular.
All works, he maintained, should be to the glory of God.

ARTHUR L. FARSTAD

During the Baroque Period, composers Johann Sebastian Bach and George Frideric Handel signed their finished scores with the words "Soli Deo Gloria" or "SDG," giving the glory for the work to God alone. Other artists like St. John of the Cross and Christoph Graupner followed suit, signing their works with SDG. These initials were the mark they gave in place of a signature, in essence offering up to God all of the accolades and notoriety the piece would garner. In an age when craftsmen and artists were publicly recognized only by their mark, this was a significant gesture.

With quotes from these classical figures and others, and historical verses from the Bible, this inspiring collection affirms that all we say, do, and produce in our daily lives is a testament to the glory of God.

God cares about us and knows all the desires of our hearts. He is as close as breathing. Let this journal inspire you to worship God in everything you do, collecting and dedicating to Him your dreams, plans, accomplishments, and prayers.

May the light of His glorious grace give you strength and shine through all aspects of your life. To God alone be the glory.

Friendships, family ties, the companionship of little children, an autumn forest flung in prodigality against a deep blue sky, the intricate design and haunting fragrance of a flower, the counterpoint of a Bach fugue or the melodic line of a Beethoven sonata, the fluted note of birdsong, the glowing glory of a sunset: the world is aflame with things of eternal moment.

E. MARGARET CLARKSON

_____

_____

_____

_____

_____

_____

_____

_____

_____

_____

_____

_____

_____

_____

_____

_____

For of Him and through Him and to Him are all things,
to whom be glory forever. Amen.

ROMANS 11:36 NKJV

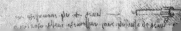

All glory and honor be unto Him in whom are comprehended all the blessings whereby God has enriched His people in time and in eternity.

CHARLES H. SPURGEON

Bless the LORD, O my soul....
Who crowns you with lovingkindness and tender mercies,
Who satisfies your mouth with good things,
So that your youth is renewed like the eagle's.

PSALM 103:1–5 NKJV

Music expresses that which cannot be put into words
and that which cannot remain silent.

VICTOR HUGO

_____

_____

_____

_____

_____

_____

_____

_____

_____

_____

_____

_____

_____

_____

_____

_____

Come, let us sing for joy to the LORD; let us shout aloud
to the Rock of our salvation. Let us come before him with thanksgiving
and extol him with music and song.

PSALM 95:1–2 NIV

Let us begin from this moment to acknowledge Him in all our ways and do everything, whatsoever we do, as service to Him and for His glory, depending upon Him alone for wisdom and strength and sweetness and patience.

HANNAH WHITALL SMITH

The LORD will guide you always; he will satisfy your needs
in a sun-scorched land and will strengthen your frame.
You will be like a well-watered garden, like a spring whose waters never fail.

ISAIAH 58:11 NIV

We have a Father in heaven who is almighty, who loves His children as He loves His only-begotten Son, and whose very joy and delight it is to...help them at all times and under all circumstances.

GEORGE MUELLER

Let us draw near with confidence to the throne of grace, so that we may receive mercy and find grace to help in time of need.

HEBREWS 4:16 NASB

All the world is an utterance of the Almighty. Its countless beauties, its exquisite adaptations, all speak to you of Him.

PHILLIPS BROOKS

Worship the LORD in the splendor of his holiness.

PSALM 96:9 NIV

Lord, I am no longer my own, but Yours. Put me to what You will, rank me with whom You will. Let me be employed by You or laid aside for You, exalted for You or brought low by You. Let me have all things, let me have nothing, I freely and heartily yield all things to Your pleasure and disposal.... You are mine and I am Yours.

JOHN WESLEY

Not unto us, O LORD, not unto us,
But to Your name give glory.

PSALM 115:1 NKJV

The wonder of our Lord is that He is so accessible to us
in the common things of our lives: the cup of water...
welcoming children into our arms...fellowship over a meal...giving thanks.

NANCIE CARMICHAEL

_____

_____

_____

_____

_____

_____

_____

_____

_____

_____

_____

_____

_____

_____

_____

_____

_____

_____

_____

Taking the child in his arms, [Jesus] said to them, "Whoever welcomes
one of these little children in my name welcomes me; and whoever
welcomes me does not welcome me but the one who sent me."

MARK 9:36–37 NIV

Lord, help me do great things as though they were little,
since I do them with Your powers; and help me to do little things
as though they were great, because I do them in Your Name.

BLAISE PASCAL

May Jesus himself and God our Father, who reached out in love
and surprised you with gifts of unending help and confidence,
put a fresh heart in you, invigorate your work, enliven your speech.

2 THESSALONIANS 2:16–17 MSG

There is nothing but God's grace. We walk upon it; we breathe it;
we live and die by it; it makes the nails and axles of the universe.

ROBERT LOUIS STEVENSON

God is able to make all grace abound to you, so that always having all
sufficiency in everything, you may have an abundance for every good deed.

2 CORINTHIANS 9:8 NASB

A life spent in brushing clothes and washing crockery and sweeping floors—a life which the proud of the earth would have treated as the dust under their feet; a life spent at the clerk's desk; a life spent in the narrow shop; a life spent in the laborer's hut, may yet be a life so ennobled by God's loving mercy that for the sake of it a king might gladly yield his crown.

FREDERICK WILLIAM FARRAR

I have come that they may have life,
and that they may have it more abundantly.

JOHN 10:10 NKJV

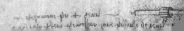

Before me, even as behind, God is, and all is well.

JOHN GREENLEAF WHITTIER

You are the light of the world. A town built on a hill cannot be hidden.
Neither do people light a lamp and put it under a bowl. Instead they
put it on its stand, and it gives light to everyone in the house.
In the same way, let your light shine before others, that they
may see your good deeds and glorify your Father in heaven.

MATTHEW 5:14–16 NIV

God's holy beauty comes near you like a spiritual scent,
and it stirs your drowsing soul.... He creates in you the desire
to find Him and run after Him—to follow wherever He leads you,
and to press peacefully against His heart wherever He is.

JOHN OF THE CROSS

You will call on me and come and pray to me, and I will listen to you.

You will seek me and find me when you seek me with all your heart.

JEREMIAH 29:12–13 NIV

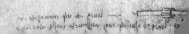

Our vocation is an asset to prayer because our work becomes prayer.
It is prayer in action. The artist, the novelist, the surgeon, the plumber,
the secretary, the lawyer, the homemaker, the farmer, the teacher—
all are praying by offering their work up to God.

RICHARD J. FOSTER

_____

_____

_____

_____

_____

_____

_____

_____

_____

_____

_____

_____

_____

_____

_____

_____

Take your everyday, ordinary life—your sleeping, eating, going-to-work,
and walking-around life—and place it before God as an offering.
Embracing what God does for you is the best thing you can do for him.

ROMANS 12:1 MSG

Perfection in outward conduct consists not in extraordinary things;
but in doing common things extraordinarily well. Neglect nothing;
the most trivial action may be performed to ourselves or performed to God.

LA MÉRE ANGÈLIQUE

Let the beauty of the LORD our God be upon us,
And establish the work of our hands for us.

PSALM 90:17 NKJV

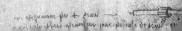

We are to simply trust God. While we trust, God can work.

GEORGE PALMER PARDINGTON

_____

_____

_____

_____

_____

_____

_____

_____

_____

_____

_____

_____

_____

_____

_____

_____

_____

The fulfillment of God's promise depends entirely on trusting God
and his way, and then simply embracing him and what he does.

ROMANS 4:16 MSG

Into Your hands, O Lord, we commend ourselves this day.
Let Your presence be with us to its close. Strengthen us to remember
that in whatsoever good work we do, we are serving You.

BOOK OF SACRAMENTS

I pray that out of his glorious riches he may strengthen you
with power through his Spirit in your inner being.

EPHESIANS 3:16 NIV

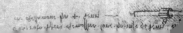

All of our Master's resources are in our hands,
entrusted to us because we are His stewards on earth.

RUTH COOK

God is the one who provides seed for the farmer and then bread to eat.
In the same way, he will provide and increase your resources
and then produce a great harvest of generosity in you.

2 CORINTHIANS 9:10 NLT

I know that [the Lord] loves me, even though I do not feel that love
as I can feel a human embrace, even though I do not hear a voice
as I hear human words of consolation.... God is greater than my senses,
greater than my thoughts, greater than my heart. I do believe
that He touches me in places that are unknown even to myself.

HENRI J. M. NOUWEN

God's Spirit touches our spirits and confirms who we really are.
We know who he is, and we know who we are: Father and children.

ROMANS 8:15–16 MSG

> [Our] fulfillment comes in knowing God's glory,
> loving Him for it, and rejoicing in it.
>
> ROBERT E. COLEMAN

May the God of hope fill you with all joy and peace
as you trust in him, so that you may overflow with hope.

ROMANS 15:13 NIV

I would teach children music, physics, and philosophy; but most importantly
music, for the patterns in music and all the arts are the keys to learning.

PLATO

_____

_____

_____

_____

_____

_____

_____

_____

_____

_____

_____

_____

_____

_____

_____

_____

The peace of God, which surpasses all understanding,
will guard your hearts and minds through Christ Jesus.

PHILIPPIANS 4:7 NKJV

Let us begin from this moment to acknowledge Him in all our ways and do everything, whatsoever we do, as service to Him and for His glory, depending upon Him alone for wisdom and strength and sweetness and patience.

HANNAH WHITALL SMITH

_____

_____

_____

_____

_____

_____

_____

_____

_____

_____

_____

_____

_____

_____

_____

_____

_____

We ask God to give you...spiritual wisdom and understanding.
Then the way you live will always honor and please the Lord,
and your lives will produce every kind of good fruit.

COLOSSIANS 1:9–10 NLT

Life from the Center is a life of unhurried peace and power.
It is simple. It is serene.... We need not get frantic. He is at the helm.
And when our little day is done, we lie down quietly in peace, for all is well.

THOMAS R. KELLY

I will both lie down in peace, and sleep;
for You alone, O LORD, make me dwell in safety.

PSALM 4:8 NKJV

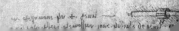

To do even the most humbling tasks to the glory of God
takes the Almighty God Incarnate working in us.

OSWALD CHAMBERS

Delight yourself in the LORD
and he will give you the desires of your heart.

PSALM 37:4 ESV

God is within all things, but not included; outside all things,
but not excluded; above all things, but not beyond their reach.

GREGORY I

_____

_____

_____

_____

_____

_____

_____

_____

_____

_____

_____

_____

_____

_____

_____

_____

_____

_____

_____

_____

_____

_____

_____

_____

_____

_____

_____

_____

_____

_____

_____

_____

_____

_____

Yours, LORD, is the greatness and the power and the glory
and the majesty and the splendor, for everything in heaven
and earth is yours.... You are exalted as head over all.

1 CHRONICLES 29:11 NIV

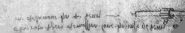

I was obliged to be industrious.
Whoever is equally industrious will succeed equally well.

JOHANN SEBASTIAN BACH

_____

_____

_____

_____

_____

_____

_____

_____

_____

_____

_____

_____

_____

_____

_____

_____

I am the vine, you are the branches. He who abides in Me, and I in him,
bears much fruit; for without Me you can do nothing.

JOHN 15:5 NKJV

When I wished to sing of love, it turned to sorrow.
And when I wished to sing of sorrow, it was transformed for me into love.

FRANZ SCHUBERT

_____

_____

_____

_____

_____

_____

_____

_____

_____

_____

_____

_____

_____

_____

_____

_____

Be of good courage, and He shall strengthen your heart,
all you who hope in the LORD.

PSALM 31:24 NKJV

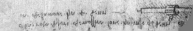

Have you ever thought that in every action of grace in your heart
you have the whole omnipotence of God engaged to bless you?

ANDREW MURRAY

From his abundance we have all received one gracious blessing after another.

JOHN 1:16 NLT

The most glorious promises of God are generally fulfilled
in such a wondrous manner that He steps forth to save us
at a time when there is the least appearance of it.

C. H. VON BOGATZKY

All the promises of God find their Yes in him.

That is why it is through him that we utter our Amen to God for his glory.

2 CORINTHIANS 1:20 ESV

God still draws near to us in the ordinary, commonplace, everyday experiences and places.... He comes in surprising ways.

HENRY GARIEPY

I have set the LORD always before me;
because He is at my right hand I shall not be moved.

PSALM 16:8 NKJV

The chief purpose of life, for any of us, is to increase according to our capacity our knowledge of God by all means we have, and to be moved by it to praise and thanks.

J.R.R. TOLKIEN

The generous will prosper; those who refresh others
will themselves be refreshed.

PROVERBS 11:25 NLT

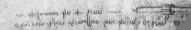

I did think I did see all heaven before me and the great God Himself.

GEORGE FRIDERIC HANDEL

_____

_____

_____

_____

_____

_____

_____

_____

_____

_____

_____

_____

_____

_____

_____

As we have heard, so we have seen in the city of the LORD Almighty,
in the city of our God: God makes her secure forever.

PSALM 48:8 NIV

It is a mistake to think that the practice of my art has become easy to me.

WOLFGANG AMADEUS MOZART

_____

_____

_____

_____

_____

_____

_____

_____

_____

_____

_____

_____

_____

_____

_____

_____

_____

_____

The reward for humility and fear of the LORD is riches and honor and life.

PROVERBS 22:4 ESV

If a man is called a streetsweeper, he should sweep streets even as Michelangelo painted or Beethoven composed music or Shakespeare wrote poetry. He should sweep streets so well that all the hosts of heaven and earth will pause to say, "Here lived a great streetsweeper who did his job well."

MARTIN LUTHER KING JR.

_____

_____

_____

_____

_____

_____

_____

_____

_____

_____

_____

_____

_____

_____

_____

Whatever you do, work at it with all your heart, as working for the Lord,
not for human masters, since you know that you will receive an inheritance
from the Lord as a reward. It is the Lord Christ you are serving.

COLOSSIANS 3:23–24 NIV

Our Creator would never have made such lovely days,
and have given us the deep hearts to enjoy them, above and beyond
all thought, unless we were meant to be immortal.

NATHANIEL HAWTHORNE

Honor and majesty surround him; strength and beauty fill his sanctuary.

PSALM 96:6 NLT

God gave me my gifts. I will do all I can to show Him
how grateful I am to Him.

GRACE LIVINGSTON HILL

_____

_____

_____

_____

_____

_____

_____

_____

_____

_____

_____

_____

_____

_____

_____

God has given each of you a gift from his great variety of spiritual gifts.
Use them well to serve one another.

1 PETER 4:10 NLT

Music is the shorthand of emotion.

LEO TOLSTOY

Blessed are the people who know the joyful sound!
They walk, O LORD, in the light of Your countenance.
In Your name they rejoice all day long,
And in Your righteousness they are exalted.

PSALM 89:15–16 NKJV

Have a purpose in life and, having it, throw into your work
such strength of mind and muscle as God has given you.

THOMAS CARLYLE

_____

_____

_____

_____

_____

_____

_____

_____

_____

_____

_____

_____

_____

_____

_____

_____

I can do all this through him who gives me strength.

PHILIPPIANS 4:13 NIV

When we commit a predicament, a possibility, a person to God in genuine confidence, we do not merely step aside and tap our foot until God comes through.... We remain in contact with God in gratitude and praise.

EUGENIA PRICE

Give thanks to the LORD, for he is good!

His faithful love endures forever.

1 CHRONICLES 16:34 NLT

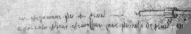

I play the notes as they are written, but it is God who makes the music.

JOHANN SEBASTIAN BACH

_____

_____

_____

_____

_____

_____

_____

_____

_____

_____

_____

_____

_____

_____

_____

_____

_____

_____

_____

_____

_____

_____

_____

_____

_____

_____

_____

_____

_____

_____

It is clear to us, friends, that God not only loves you very much
but also has put His hand on you for something special.

1 THESSALONIANS 1:4 MSG

Those who know God have great contentment in God. There is no peace like the peace of those whose minds are possessed with full assurance that they have known God and God has known them and that this relationship guarantees God's favor to them in life, through death, and on forever.

J. I. PACKER

Godliness with contentment is great gain.

1 TIMOTHY 6:6 NIV

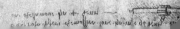

There was no one near to confuse me, so I was forced to become original.

JOSEPH HAYDN

_____

_____

_____

_____

_____

_____

_____

_____

_____

_____

_____

_____

_____

_____

_____

Do not conform to the pattern of this world,
but be transformed by the renewing of your mind.

ROMANS 12:2 NIV

The sun...in its full glory, either at rising or setting—this, and many other like blessings we enjoy daily; and for the most of them, because they are so common, most men forget to pay their praises. But let not us.

ISAAK WALTON

I pray that you…know this love that surpasses knowledge—
that you may be filled to the measure of all the fullness of God.

EPHESIANS 3:17, 19 NIV

In whatever [God] does in the course of our lives, He gives us,
through the experience, some power to help others.

ELISABETH ELLIOT

_____

_____

_____

_____

_____

_____

_____

_____

_____

_____

_____

_____

_____

_____

_____

_____

He comforts us in all our troubles so that we can comfort others. When they are troubled, we will be able to give them the same comfort God has given us.

2 CORINTHIANS 1:4 NLT

God is glorified not only by His glory being seen, but by its being rejoiced in.
When those that see it delight in it, God is more glorified than if they only
see it. His glory is then received by the whole soul.

JONATHAN EDWARDS

Rejoice always, pray continually, give thanks in all circumstances;
for this is God's will for you in Christ Jesus.

1 THESSALONIANS 5:16–18 NIV

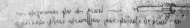

I think of faith as a kind of whistling in the dark because, in much the same way, it helps to give us courage and to hold the shadows at bay. To whistle in the dark...demonstrate[s], if only to ourselves, that not even the dark can quite overcome our trust in the ultimate triumph of the Living Light.

FREDERICK BUECHNER

_____

_____

_____

_____

_____

_____

_____

_____

_____

_____

_____

_____

_____

_____

_____

_____

_____

_____

You light my lamp; the LORD my God illumines my darkness.

PSALM 18:28 NASB

The very act of prayer honors God and gives glory to God,
for it confesses that God is what He is.

CHARLES KINGSLEY

The Lord is righteous in all his ways and faithful in all he does.
The Lord is near to all who call on him, to all who call on him in truth.

PSALM 145:17–18 NIV

For God loves and enjoys us—and the Divine Will wants us to love
and enjoy God in return and rest in this strength. And all shall be well.

JULIAN OF NORWICH

_____

_____

_____

_____

_____

_____

_____

_____

_____

_____

_____

_____

_____

_____

_____

_____

_____

_____

_____

You shall walk in all the ways which the LORD your God has commanded
you, that you may live and that it may be well with you.

DEUTERONOMY 5:33 NKJV

From the heart of God comes the strongest rhythm—the rhythm of love.
Without His love reverberating in us, whatever we do will come across
like a noisy gong or a clanging symbol. And so the work of the human heart,
it seems to me, is to listen for that music and pick up on its rhythms.

KEN GIRE

If I could speak all the languages of earth and of angels,
but didn't love others, I would only be a noisy gong or a clanging cymbal....
Love never gives up, never loses faith, is always hopeful,
and endures through every circumstance.

1 CORINTHIANS 13:1, 7 NLT

Life is what we are alive to. It is not length but breadth....
Be alive to...goodness, kindness, purity, love, history,
poetry, music, flowers, stars, God, and eternal hope.

MALTBIE D. BABCOCK

On the inside, where God is making new life,
not a day goes by without his unfolding grace.

2 CORINTHIANS 4:16–17 MSG

Music is a higher revelation than all wisdom and philosophy.

JOHANNES VAN BEETHOVEN

_____

_____

_____

_____

_____

_____

_____

_____

_____

_____

_____

_____

_____

_____

_____

_____

_____

_____

Wisdom from above is first of all pure. It is also peace loving,
gentle at all times, and willing to yield to others. It is full of mercy
and the fruit of good deeds. It shows no favoritism and is always sincere.

JAMES 3:17 NLT

We walk without fear, full of hope and courage and strength
to do His will, waiting for the endless good which He is always
giving as fast as He can get us able to take it in.

GEORGE MACDONALD

_____

_____

_____

_____

_____

_____

_____

_____

_____

_____

_____

_____

_____

_____

_____

_____

_____

The Lord longs to be gracious to you; therefore he will rise up
to show you compassion. For the Lord is a God of justice.
Blessed are all who wait for him!

ISAIAH 30:18 NIV

The colored sunsets and starry heavens, the beautiful mountains
and the shining seas, the fragrant woods and painted flowers,
are not half so beautiful as a soul that is serving Jesus out of love
in the wear and tear of common, unpoetic life.

FREDERICK W. FABER

_____
_____
_____
_____
_____
_____
_____
_____
_____
_____
_____
_____
_____
_____
_____
_____

Dear friend, I pray that you may enjoy good health and that all
may go well with you, even as your soul is getting along well.

3 JOHN 1:2 NIV

What a wonderful thing it is to be sure of one's faith! How wonderful
to be a member of the evangelical church, which preaches the free grace
of God through Christ as the hope of sinners! If we were to rely
on our works—my God, what would become of us?

GEORGE FRIDERIC HANDEL

_____

_____

_____

_____

_____

_____

_____

_____

_____

_____

_____

_____

_____

_____

The LORD is my light and my salvation; whom shall I fear?
The LORD is the strength of my life; of whom shall I be afraid?

PSALM 27:1 NKJV

No matter what our occupations are—musician, garbage collector,
football coach—when we come to Christ, we all become
Christian workers first; musicians, garbage collectors,
or football coaches, second. Whatever our "callings,"
we are preeminently called to serve Christ in and through our work.

BEN PATTERSON

_____

_____

_____

_____

_____

_____

_____

_____

_____

_____

_____

_____

_____

_____

Each person should live as a believer in whatever situation the Lord
has assigned to them, just as God has called them.

1 CORINTHIANS 7:17 NIV

The final aim and reason of all music is nothing other than
the glorification of God and the refreshment of the spirit.

JOHANN SEBASTIAN BACH

_____

_____

_____

_____

_____

_____

_____

_____

_____

_____

_____

_____

_____

_____

_____

_____

_____

_____

Let everything that breathes sing praises to the LORD! Praise the LORD!

PSALM 150:6 NLT

As sure as it is our duty to look wholly unto God in our prayers,
so sure is it that it is our duty to live wholly unto God in our lives.

WILLIAM LAW

_____

_____

_____

_____

_____

_____

_____

_____

_____

_____

_____

_____

_____

_____

_____

_____

_____

_____

_____

_____

_____

_____

_____

_____

_____

_____

_____

_____

_____

_____

_____

_____

_____

_____

_____

Our Father in heaven, hallowed be Your name. Your kingdom come.
Your will be done on earth as it is in heaven. Give us this day our daily bread.
And forgive us our debts, as we forgive our debtors. And do not lead
us into temptation, but deliver us from the evil one. For Yours
is the kingdom and the power and the glory forever. Amen.

MATTHEW 6:9–13 NKJV

[God] delights to meet the faith of one who looks up to Him and says,
"Lord, You know that I cannot do this—but I believe that You can!"

AMY CARMICHAEL

_____

_____

_____

_____

_____

_____

_____

_____

_____

_____

_____

_____

_____

_____

_____

_____

_____

He led me to a place of safety; he rescued me because he delights in me.

2 SAMUEL 22:20 NLT

God does not so much want us to do things as to let people see what He can do. God is not looking for extraordinary characters as His instruments, but He is looking for humble instruments through whom He can be honored throughout the ages.

A. B. SIMPSON

_____

_____

_____

_____

_____

_____

_____

_____

_____

_____

_____

_____

You are a chosen people.... God's very own possession.
As a result, you can show others the goodness of God,
for he called you out of the darkness into his wonderful light.

1 PETER 2:9 NLT

That is God's call to us—simply to be people who are content
to live close to Him and to renew the kind of life in which
the closeness is felt and experienced.

THOMAS MERTON

You have made known to me the path of life; you will fill me with joy
in your presence, with eternal pleasures at your right hand.

PSALM 16:11 NIV

What you are doing I may not be able to do.... What I am doing you may not be able to do.... But all of us together are doing something beautiful for God.

MOTHER TERESA

There are varieties of gifts, but the same Spirit; and there are varieties
of service, but the same Lord; and there are varieties of activities,
but it is the same God who empowers them all in everyone.

1 CORINTHIANS 12:4–6 ESV

If we have been learning to worship God and to trust Him,
the crisis will reveal that we will go to the breaking point
and not break in our confidence in Him.

OSWALD CHAMBERS

I trust in the LORD.
I will be glad and rejoice in your unfailing love,
for you have seen my troubles,
and you care about the anguish of my soul.

PSALM 31:6–7 NLT

The serene beauty of a holy life is the most powerful influence
in the world next to the power of God.

BLAISE PASCAL

_____

_____

_____

_____

_____

_____

_____

_____

_____

_____

_____

_____

_____

_____

_____

_____

Fear-of-GOD is life itself, a full life, and serene.

PROVERBS 19:23 MSG

To send light into the darkness of men's hearts—
such is the duty of the artist.

ROBERT SCHUMANN

Because of God's tender mercy, the morning light from heaven
is about to break upon us, to give light to those who sit in darkness...
and to guide us to the path of peace.

LUKE 1:78–79 NLT

The place where God calls you to is the place where
your deep gladness and the world's deep hunger meet.

FREDERICK BUECHNER

_____

_____

_____

_____

_____

_____

_____

_____

_____

_____

_____

_____

_____

_____

_____

_____

_____

Blessed are those who hunger and thirst for righteousness,
for they shall be satisfied.

MATTHEW 5:6 NASB

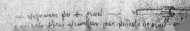

By reading of Scripture I am so renewed that all nature seems renewed
around me and with me. The sky seems to be a purer, a cooler blue,
the trees a deeper green, light is sharper on the outlines of the forest
and the hills and the whole world is charged with the glory of God.

THOMAS MERTON

_____

_____

_____

_____

_____

_____

_____

_____

_____

_____

_____

_____

_____

_____

_____

See, I am doing a new thing! Now it springs up; do you not perceive it?
I am making a way in the wilderness and streams in the wasteland.

ISAIAH 43:19 NIV

The fruit of our placing all things in His hands
is the presence of His abiding peace in our hearts.

HANNAH WHITALL SMITH

I will say of the LORD, "He is my refuge and my fortress;
my God, in Him I will trust."

PSALM 91:2 NKJV

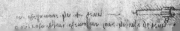

Without craftsmanship, inspiration is a mere reed shaken in the wind.

JOHANNES BRAHMS

In his grace, God has given us different gifts for doing certain things well....
If your gift is serving others, serve them well. If you are a teacher, teach
well.... And if you have a gift for showing kindness to others, do it gladly.

ROMANS 12:6-8 NLT

Be such a person, and live such a life, that if every one were such as you,
and every life a life such as yours, this earth would be God's paradise.

PHILLIPS BROOKS

_____

_____

_____

_____

_____

_____

_____

_____

_____

_____

_____

_____

_____

_____

_____

_____

_____

_____

_____

Live out your God-created identity. Live generously
and graciously toward others, the way God lives toward you.

MATTHEW 5:48 MSG

It is a great consolation for me to remember that the Lord,
to whom I had drawn near in humble and childlike faith, has suffered
and died for me, and that He will look on me in love and compassion.

WOLFGANG AMADEUS MOZART

_____

_____

_____

_____

_____

_____

_____

_____

_____

_____

_____

_____

_____

_____

_____

_____

Humble yourselves in the sight of the Lord, and He will lift you up.

JAMES 4:10 NKJV

Know by the light of faith that God is present,
and be content with directing all your actions toward Him.

BROTHER LAWRENCE

_____

_____

_____

_____

_____

_____

_____

_____

_____

_____

_____

_____

_____

_____

_____

_____

If I rise on the wings of the dawn, if I settle on the far side of the sea,
even there your hand will guide me, your right hand will hold me fast.

PSALM 139:9–10 NIV

If Christ lives in us, controlling our personalities,
we will leave glorious marks on the lives we touch.
Not because of our lovely characters, but because of His.

EUGENIA PRICE

_____

_____

_____

_____

_____

_____

_____

_____

_____

_____

_____

_____

_____

_____

_____

_____

We love Him because He first loved us.

1 JOHN 4:19 NKJV

God guides us.... He leads us step by step, from event to event.
Only afterward...do we experience the feeling of having been led
without knowing it, the feeling that God has mysteriously guided us.

PAUL TOURNIER

F

J

E

You guide me with your counsel, leading me to a glorious destiny.

PSALM 73:24 NLT

God's timing is rarely our timing. But far better than we do, He numbers
our days and knows our moments and our hours. Our task is to trust.

OS GUINNESS

_____

_____

_____

_____

_____

_____

_____

_____

_____

_____

_____

_____

_____

_____

_____

_____

_____

_____

_____

_____

_____

_____

_____

_____

_____

_____

_____

_____

_____

_____

_____

_____

_____

_____

_____

Blessed is the one who trusts in the LORD.

PROVERBS 16:20 NIV

Music gives a soul to the universe, wings to the mind,
flight to the imagination and life to everything.

PLATO

_____

_____

_____

_____

_____

_____

_____

_____

_____

_____

_____

_____

_____

_____

_____

_____

_____

_____

_____

_____

_____

_____

_____

_____

_____

_____

_____

_____

_____

_____

Whoever believes in me, as Scripture has said,
rivers of living water will flow from within them.

JOHN 7:38 NIV

Be assured, if you walk with Him and look to Him
and expect help from Him, He will never fail you.

GEORGE MUELLER

Because of the LORD's great love we are not consumed,
for his compassions never fail.

LAMENTATIONS 3:22 NIV

I'm a little pencil in the hands of a loving God
who is writing a love letter to the world.

MOTHER TERESA

You, my brothers and sisters, were called to be free....
Use your freedom to...serve one another humbly in love.

GALATIANS 5:13 NIV

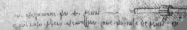

[Amy Carmichael's] great longing was to have a "single eye" for the glory of God. Whatever might blur the vision God had given her of His work, whatever could distract or deceive or tempt her to seek anything but the Lord Jesus Himself she tried to eliminate.

ELISABETH ELLIOT

We know that all things work together for good to those who love God,
to those who are the called according to His purpose.

ROMANS 8:28 NKJV

Ellie Claire® Gift & Paper Expressions
Brentwood, TN 37027
EllieClaire.com
Ellie Claire is registered trademark of Worthy Media, Inc.

Soli Deo Gloria: To God Alone Be the Glory
© 2015 by Ellie Claire
Published by Ellie Claire, an imprint of Worthy Publishing Group,
a division of Worthy Media, Inc.

ISBN 978-1-63326-058-0

Scripture quotations are taken from the following sources: The Holy Bible, New International Version®, NIV® Copyright © 1973, 1978, 1984, 2011 by Biblica, Inc.® All rights reserved worldwide. The Holy Bible, New King James Version® (NKJV). Copyright © 1982 by Thomas Nelson, Inc. The Holy Bible, English Standard Version® (ESV®), copyright © 2001 by Crossway Bibles, a publishing ministry of Good News Publishers. The New American Standard Bible® (NASB), Copyright © 1960, 1962, 1963, 1968, 1971, 1972, 1973, 1975, 1977, 1995 by The Lockman Foundation. The Holy Bible, New Living Translation (NLT) copyright © 1996, 2004, 2007 by Tyndale House Foundation. Used by permission of Tyndale House Publishers Inc., Carol Stream, Illinois 60188. *The Message* (MSG). Copyright © 1993, 1994, 1995, 1996, 2000, 2001, 2002. Used by permission of NavPress Publishing Group. All rights reserved.

Excluding Scripture verses and deity pronouns, in some quotations references to men and masculine pronouns have been replaced with gender-neutral or feminine references. Additionally, in some quotations we have carefully updated verb forms and wording that may distract modern readers.

Stock or custom editions of Ellie Claire titles may be purchased in bulk for educational, business, ministry, fund-raising, or sales promotional use. For information, please e-mail info@EllieClaire.com.

Compiled by Barbara Farmer
Cover and interior design by Gearbox | studiogearbox.com

Printed in China

1 2 3 4 5 6 7 8 9 – 20 19 18 17 16 15